# SURPRISING MYSELF

*by*
## Jean Fritz

*photographs by*
## Andrea Fritz Pfleger

 Richard C. Owen Publishers, Inc.
Katonah, New York

## Meet the Author titles

Verna Aardema  *A Bookworm Who Hatched*
Jean Fritz  *Surprising Myself*
Lee Bennett Hopkins  *The Writing Bug*
Rafe Martin  *A Storyteller's Story*
Cynthia Rylant  *Best Wishes*
Jane Yolen  *A Letter from Phoenix Farm*

Text copyright © 1992 by Jean Fritz
Photographs copyright © 1992 by Andrea Fritz Pfleger

Richard C. Owen Publishers, Inc.
135 Katonah Avenue
Katonah, New York 10536

Library of Congress Cataloging-in-Publication Data

Fritz, Jean.
  Surprising myself / by Jean Fritz : photographs by Andrea Fritz
Pfleger.
    p.  cm. — (Meet the author)
  Summary: Fritz, a well-known author of books for young people,
describes her daily life and the way she writes.
  ISBN 1-878450-37-9 ( hardcover )
  1. Fritz, Jean — Biography — Juvenile literature. 2. Authors,
American — 20th century — Biography — Juvenile literature.
3. Authorship — Juvenile literature.  [1. Fritz, Jean.  2. Authors,
American.]  I. Pfleger, Andrea Fritz, ill.  II. Title.
III. Series : Meet the author (Katonah, N. Y.)
PS3556. R5697Z474  1992
813 ' . 54 — dc20
[ B ]                                                    93-12001

The text type was set in Caslon 540.
Editor-in-Chief Janice Boland
Production Manager Amy J. Haggblom

Printed in the United States of America

9 8 7 6 5 4 3 2 1

To my photographer

I like to explore. I've always liked to explore.
I grew up in China beside the Yangtse River,
where I went exploring every chance I had.
I loved the Yangtse River,
and when I wrote poetry as a child,
the Yangtse River often wound its way into it.
Now I live in Dobbs Ferry, New York,
beside the Hudson River, which I love, too.

The nice things about exploring are that
you never know whom you'll meet
and you never know what surprises you'll find.

Once I found a chain on a beach.
It looks so old I like to imagine
it came from a Spanish sailing ship.

Stories often come as surprises, too.
One time when I was exploring the coast of Alaska,
I had a chance to dig for gold.

A real gold digger lent me a shovel.
I didn't find any gold,
but I did find a story about an Alaskan island.
I called it "There is an Island"
and you can find it in *The Big Book for Peace*.

I never know when or where I'm going to find a story.
I may look as if I'm reading,
but I'm really dashing through history, exploring!
When I was in school
all I ever learned about history
was facts and events.
I wanted to know about the real people
who lived in those times,
so I decided to find out about them myself.

Sometimes it seems as if a person from long ago
steps out from a page and speaks to me.
Then I know I have to write another book.

First I go to the library
and read, read, read, read.
Of course, I make notes as I go along.
Then I travel to the places
where my characters lived
so I can get to know them on their own home ground.

When I was writing my book *The Great Little Madison*,
I went to James Madison's home in Virginia.
I took notes on everything I saw.
I stood on the same steps where he once stood
and looked out at his lovely plantation.
I imagined him doing the same thing.

One day I read a magazine article about a man
who sailed from Ireland to America in a leather boat,
just as Saint Brendan is said to have done long ago.
I knew I had to write Saint Brendan's story,
and off I went to Ireland
to talk to the people there about him.
I explored the very spot
where Saint Brendan was supposed to have set sail.
I called my book
*Brendan the Navigator: A History Mystery.*

After I travel, I go home to write.
I write in longhand first.
I cross out as I go along,
rewrite, and cross out again.
I can never seem to find
the right words the first time.

At the end of every writing day
I go to my word processor
and type up what I've written.
I'm lucky if I have two pages.

Even so, I've managed to write
more than fifteen stories
about historical people so far.

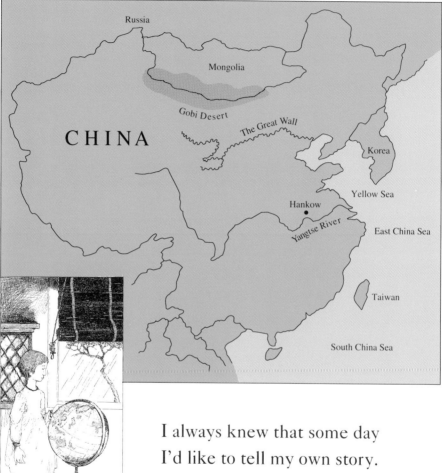

I always knew that some day
I'd like to tell my own story.
My Chinese world was so different
from my American world
I wanted to put down my childhood memories
so there would be no chance of losing them.
I called that book *Homesick: My Own Story*.

Then, in 1983, I went back to my hometown in China.
That was one of my most exciting trips.
I found my old house!
I kept stopping to talk to people in the street—
in Chinese, of course.
*"Ni hau, ma?"* ("How are you?") I'd ask.
I visited a Chinese school and showed the children
a photograph album which the children of Dobbs Ferry
had made of their everyday life in America.
The Chinese children were so interested,
they couldn't get close enough.

Every winter I take three weeks off from my writing
to go to Virgin Gorda,
an island in the Caribbean Sea,
where I swim and snorkle
and just stare at the wonderful blue-green water.
I leave the manuscript I'm working on at home,
but that's scary!
Suppose the house should burn down!
So, before I go out of town, I put my manuscript
in the safest place I can think of—the refrigerator.
Then off I go!

When I'm on the island, I often sit on a rock
and think about Christopher Columbus,
who sailed past for the first time in 1493.
Columbus loved the Caribbean Islands, just as I do.
And he kept finding surprises.

On one island he found hammocks.
They were new to him.
I found a hammock, too.
I've written about Columbus a lot,
and other explorers, too.
I wrote a whole book about explorers.
I called it *Around the World in 100 Years*.

I not only sit on rocks, I crawl between them.
And take time just to dream.

Sometimes I go exploring with my husband Michael,
my daughter Andrea, and her husband Frank.
Once we drove off to explore an old copper mine.

Before I leave Virgin Gorda
I take a last long look at the sea.
That look has to last me for a whole year.

When we get back from our trip,
I can't wait to see my son David and his family.
Often we arrive just in time
for his wife Carmela's birthday party.

I'm always glad to be back with my grandsons,
Michael Scott and Dan.
Of course we read together.

And Michael Scott and I build with blocks.

Then it's back to work.
I know my manuscript
is waiting for me in the refrigerator.
I work long hours and try to write
at least one book a year.
When I feel my manuscript is finished,
I send it to my editor to read.
Then off I go again, exploring.
There's no telling what surprises I'll find!

## Some Other Books by Jean Fritz

*Shh! We're Writing the Constitution*; *What's the Big Idea, Ben Franklin?*; *Will You Sign Here, John Hancock?*

## About the Photographer

Andrea Fritz Pfleger enjoys gardening, reading, and boating on the Hudson River. She and her husband Frank live on a lake in New York with their four house cats and three barn cats.

## Acknowledgments

Illustration on page 7 from *Where Do You Think You're Going, Christopher Columbus?* illustrations © 1980 by Margot Tomes. Illustration on page 11 from *George Washington's Breakfast*, illustrations © 1969 by Paul Galdone. Illustrations on page 17 from *Where Was Patrick Henry on the 29th of May?* illustrations © 1975 by Margot Tomes, from *Why Don't You Get a Horse, Sam Adams?* illustrations © 1974 by Trina Schart Hyman, and from *Can't You Make Them Behave, King George?* illustrations © 1977 by Tomie dePaola. Illustration on page 18 from *Homesick*, illustrations © 1982 by Margot Tomes. Permission granted by G.P. Putnam's Sons and Coward, McCann & Geohegan. Photographs on pages 1, 8, 9, 13, 14, 19, and the back cover courtesy of Michael Fritz. Photographs on pages 3, 15, and 32 courtesy of Frank Pfleger. Photograph on page 4 courtesy of Jean Fritz.